FOREWORD

This book is the preparation of stepping out on faith.

"Church tonight babe" I always found every excuse not to go to the house of God. Sometimes I felt like a hypocrite. You know go to Church to please someone else. But tonight I was energetic to be in the house of the Lord. Maybe it was the new car that I wanted to show off! Or the blazer that I picked up from Unique's. Whatever the case was Teri and myself was there front and center for all to see.

I sat back and listened to the introduction of the speaker for the night. The dark skin guy wearing the dark shades and the tailored Black suit stepped to the Pulpit was energized from the gate;

"You brother!" He whispered as he made his way down the aisle; The Holy Spirit just told me to tell you that there is about to be a Shift in your life. God is about to give you your life back!" He then used two fingers to tap me back into the seat. I sat there with tears flowing down my face.

He told a young lady; "God was just testing you and He said to tell you that you have passed the test. When you thought you needed what your heart desired you weren't ready for it. But He's about to shower you with more than you ever desired." The young lady began to Shout and Praise dance for the next twenty minutes.

This guy I later learned was a Prophet that spoke things into existence things that a person could have only shared with God Himself. Many people were blessed this night. Even my Pastor, Pastor Bellamy of the Church who he told must make some changes involving the removal of ones that held titles in the Church. Scary but if God says, she must adhere to this.

The Shift
"Success is not a Given"

By: Zachery Hoagland

Chapter One

As Teri and I lie across our king size bed watching Medea's Family Reunion, Teri looks at me and says;

"Babe as I watch this movie I can really see you behind the scenes as the writer of this script."

"Sweetie the sad thing is I have a library of books that can be converted into movies." I thought to myself. But more importantly I began to think about the similarity I had with the life that Tyler Perry lived before he became who is he today.

Similarities like how the car that I drove everyday became Home for months. The eating out of the garbage. To subjecting myself to someone else's means of manipulation. The ones that showed that they had your best interest was later revealed as the worst breed to be connected to. The countless NOs that that I used as motivation to get to that Yes!

I sat back thinking about all the different books that I've written that touches on these heartfelt topics.

My one book titled "Jack Hoagalino" talks about the womanizing characteristics that were passed down from generation to generation. From the comedians that raised me, to the conniving manipulators that were so relevant to my later lifestyle. How the ones that knew no better spoon fed me this as if it were the next big thing to leading a profound life. Not to mention the blessings that the streets robbed me for.

I was given ample opportunity to educate myself way before the drugs, the prisons and institutions got a hold of me and latched onto me.

Kay kay's voice interrupted my thoughts;

"Well you know Tyler Perry is right in Atlanta?" Kay kay chimed. She was now holding her phone in the palm of her hand. She then showed me two studios that were I assume in the heart of down town Atlanta, Georgia. Kay kay was who she was. Always made things sound so reachable. She has no problem bringing things to the forefront.

Whatever you needed Kay kay was your go to person. Place of residence? Ask Kay kay! Discounts? Sales? Ask Kay kay! Technical difficulties? Ask Kay kay. Today Kay kay has the information that was definitely needed.

"Bae, I have to meet this guy!" I whispered.

"I want to move to Atlanta!" Kay kay yelled with so much energy that I push the pause button on the Television. Kay kay instantly prompted thoughts of what life would be like living in Atlanta.

"Well compared to three hots and a cot, Atlanta sounds like heaven Kay kay. Uber would have to be the main source of income." I thought.

"Before we make a move like that I would need something else than to depend solely on Uber." I told her.

"Babe, said Teri, I can tell by the look in your eyes that it's time to leave Jersey. But don't let Kay kay convince you to make this move until we have at least $10,000.00 saved." That's my wife Y'all.

I grabbed my wife hands and began to pray.

"Lord I know at times I can be a little over the top with my desires. So I don't want to sound greedy. Nor do I want you to make it easy for me, but I ask that you bless my hands and aid me in getting the tools to make it to my dream! Amen."

Amen!" my wife repeated. And we left it alone.

"Get ready Tyler we're on my way." I thought. Although Kay kay was unrealistic to think that we will be on the next flight to ATL the energy she had when she spoke of this place, made thinking about the move edible. She became one of my reasons to pursue my dreams in Atlanta.

As I was speaking to my daughter my Commercial driver's license popped up in my head. Unlike the 7 times failure, I felt stronger than ever about obtaining them. Immediately after Medea's Family Reunion went off I made plans to get back in School for my CDL training. Immediately I began looking for Providence trucking school phone number.

"Pedro what's up?"

"Hey my friend" He spoke into the receiver in his German accent.

"Although you haven't heard from me in months, you already know why I'm calling." I told him. Pedro didn't care. He was about his business. (Many are called but few will be chosen) was his attitude. So to him nothing was taken personal. But still he played the role of a concerned relative, because at the end of the day it was all about the money to him. The more I failed to pass, the more money he made off me.

"My friend I was concerned about you but I knew you would eventually call." And he was right reader. I can count on one hand how many times I've Started this task without Completion. I envisioned it. I claimed it, Or I believed and received it. And by any means I'd get to it all over again.

"So have you been studying?" He asked. (Studying? I thought. PLEASE)

"No Pedro, I haven't been studying since I failed that last test."

"WELLLL I can help you to get the CDL, but it's all up to you working." He said that with uncertainty reader. And I immediately bit.

Chapter Two

That morning I made my way to Providence Driving School. As I sat waiting for the lady to finish with her client, I made sure that I had all the needed documents. After looking at my documents she informed me that my License has expired. And that I must renew before I'm able to begin my training again. From there I went to DMV.

"Howdy Sir, fill this out and jump into that line." I listened to the Officer and I finally made it to the front of this mile-long line.

After viewing my documents the clerk informed me since my license had expired, I would have to retake the test. Reader I was fuming. You talking about a test with 100 Q's and A's that I failed 7 times back to back. My thoughts were I'm here so I might as well take this test

"Good morning Sir how can I help you?" Whispered the chubby Caucasian woman who was seated behind a Chest high counter while stuffing her face with what seemed to be a cream cheese everything bagel.

"Good morning ma'am, I was told that because my CDLs expired that I would have to take the test again." Reader I was still trying to swindle that renewal without retesting. Un-fortunately, all the co-workers were all in agreement with one another.

Now seated in front of the same computer #13 that I sat in front of this time last year.

NAME: Jack Hoagalino? Yes!
BIRTH DATE: May 3, 1976? Yes!
AGE: 40? Yes! So on and so forth.

After failing once again I explained to my Teri that I didn't pass and It was back in study mode.

"Well baby cakes, you'll get it. Just go back and get it next week." My Teri was always so optimistic with me and my worth. Believe it or not reader, sometimes that push can take us above and beyond our wildest Dreams.

Chapter Three

As I walked into the aroma of the meal that was being prepared I began to think about who this woman was to me and what our purpose was.

It's those little things like coming home to a prepared meal that we as people tend to overlook. it's like we get so used to having things laid at our feet that we forget that as independent individuals we should appreciate someone taking time out of their day to think about not only making sure that we eat but slave over a stove to make sure that we eat!

"What's burning sweetheart?" My Teri just smiled as she continued to work her magic. (Whatever it was reader I couldn't wait to dive in.)

"Well is there anything that you need me to help with?"

"No Baby cakes! Just jump in the shower (Something I fight with. Lol.) and keep yourself busy until I bring your plate to you." That was fair enough reader. I pulled the stopper for the tub, ran the bath water, added Arm and Hammer Baking Soda, and a little solution from Dr. Bronner's Products.

"Pure Castile Peppermint soap!"

For all of you with sweet smelling feet and private parts, this wouldn't be for you. But the ones that has 12 hours shift days of hard work scents, this soap would be perfect for you. Anyway, as I soaked my feet I turned on the shower to let the water roll off my back.

Now I'm in my comfort zone seated at my desk, HP computer loaded and ready to be at the hands of my mercy. As I sat trying to tackle one of the most prominent projects yet I get a call.

"What uuup thhooo?!" Bmore always spoke like he was dragging his teeth. Or tongue for that matter.

"What's going on?!" I greeted.

"Yo I heard you was ready to make that mooovvve." As he spoke on it I vision how the first week would be. From what I've been hearing Atlanta was Black Wall Street. Black owned Businesses with Urban last names. Times square in Africa. So on and so forth.

"Hey, brother you from Jersey? Well I have my own store. I would love to have you set your table up or you can have a book signing at my cousin's store!"

"Yeah I'm on the count down." I confirmed. Did you ever get the dog that I need? I'm trying to get this breed off the ground asap."

"I got a dog, but I don't think you ready for that Jeep Red boy Eli!" B'more was obsessed with having bragging rights. And 90 % of the time he had all his ducks lined up. So unless you had a qualified level of resource most would be a fool to challenge his arguments. And that was on every level. From Hood gossip to Sports. Oh of course Dogs. But it was hard to take a person serious that never answers his phone and barely calls back.

"Yeah, I'm on that 95 south in two weeks." I told him.

"Yo why you moving so far away?" He asked. With my Lady's voice in my head, I paused for a minute.

"Babycakes, you talk too much. Sometimes you have to make things happen and let the viewers see the results. And although revealing my missions before they take off was my way of motivating myself. Because instead of praying for your success, people have the tendency to let the devil use them to prey on your downfall. She was right. But I just couldn't keep it to myself.

"My Lady and I just bought a house. I should get these CDLs in the next couple of weeks and have them as my back up while I chase my dream."

He became voiceless. "I wrote about me traveling to Atlanta to meet Tyler Perry. My plan is to take it to his Estate." I told him.

"To his Estate? His house?? Man Georgia is going to put your Tail under the jail. Besides you ain't getting pass that security."

"Why don't you just go to his studio?" He asked. I listened to what he had to say but leaned more to Mr. Perry and myself must have a heart to heart and that type of discussion would have to be in the comfort of his home.

If nothing else when the Police does lock me up I'm hoping that he has room in his heart for my de-termination. Maybe he will respect my arrogance. Some say I'm crazy! Maybe he'll respect my crazy.

"Okay Dream chaser" B'more laughed. Well I don't have bail money so I hope you have a stash from all of them books you moving from State to State." Although he said that in a joking manner, he was grave serious. today trying to get a dollar from a family member is like pulling teeth.

Chapter Four

Today is my Teri's day off and like every day she has, I turned my Uber account off then head home before she gets up. The highlights of having such a job is the fact that I can make my own hours and still get quality pay. I decided to contact her to see if she had a taste for anything specific.

"Are you up sweetheart?" Was the text that I sent to her phone. To No response. I sent Teri another text that went on deaf ears. After 7 texts I figured;

"Okay she must be sleep." I thought. But when I walked through the doors of our home she's wide awake singing gospel songs, praise dancing and shouting like never before while cleaning the house.

"Hey baby cakes!" She chimed as we made eye contact.

"What's up sweetie?!" I returned the greeting with a light smile attached. I then opened my arms to accept her into my embrace. It felt so good. Making it home must be the best part of the day. Well for me anyway. Because in some households going home could be a haunted situation. arguments, fusses and in most cases, knock down dragged out fights! Fortunately for me it was cheers and smiles of innocence.

"Hey Jack!" one would chime. "Hey Jackariah!" the other would whisper. "Heyyyy!" and "Heyyyy Baby cakes!" Was all I heard as I swayed through the home of them Hoagalinos.

So, like everyone else I fell right in line. When most guys would have a personal vendetta against dishes and being the one to clean them. I usually took the initiative to make things right. Tissue on the floor or in the toilet, I pick it up or flush it down the toilet. Dirty tub, guess what Jack got to work! So on and so forth!

In my household coming up as the only child for a lot of years there weren't too many chores that I wasn't introduced to and familiar with. So, I grabbed an empty pot, filled it up with hot water, Dawn dish soap and Bust them suds.

Chapter Five

"Babe are you aware of the storm that's about to hit us?" As I read the text not only did I remember assuring my Teri that I'll be home when she gets there but I forgot that we were having a big storm.

As I was reaching for the talk button to call and confirm that I was on my way another trip popped into my phone. "Dang I forgot to turn the Uber off!" I thought. After accepting the request I replied to my wife.

"Yes sweetie I'm well aware of the storm" I texted. I'll accept this last trip and make my way home." This was during the time that the PGA Tours were in different parts of New Jersey. So these trips were liable to be heading anywhere. I prayed that this one will be local.

After a five-minute ride into Summit, New Jersey I double parked outside of a Starbucks.

While waiting there with my hazards on a Jewish guy wearing prescription glasses came to the car and attempted to open the door. He was so aggressive with opening the door that the handle snapped back loud enough for me to jump. I hit the automatic locks button to release the locks. I then informed him that the door was open.

Without speaking this arrogant guy threw his suitcase (Wet suitcase!) in the back seat and attempted to climb inside. It wasn't hard to see this guy carried wealth.

"Sir let me help you with putting that in the trunk." After looking over the bridge of his glasses he growled that his bag stays with him.

"Sir maybe you misunderstood me. But the suitcase MUST go in the trunk." I said this more Stern than Howard! He sat there searching my face as if I were speaking another language. So I turned the car off and with direct eye contact I informed this cocky guy that either the bag goes in the trunk or I cancel the trip before it begins.

Like a little girl he sucked his teeth, and stomped his hard bottoms as he made his way to the back of my pretty Plum colored 3 series BMW. With a straight face inside I was filled with laughter.

I clicked the lock on the trunk and before I could get back there he had the trunk open and closed. So I spun on my heels and climbed back inside. Shortly after I swiped to start the trip. HARTSDALE, NEW YORK?!

"Dang! Dang! Dang!" I thought. Reader I never saw this coming. But I couldn't turn back now. So I began my two hour trip to upstate New York.

After hearing parts of his conversation, it confirmed that he was some type of big time record producer. If the guy wasn't wealthy, he was for sure a heavy hitter in his profession.

"Yes Mr. West, I can only go as fast as the Uber guy gets me there!" I just listened and although he was being sarcastic I focused on the trip.

Maybe 40 minutes into the trip we were fighting with the traffic that Highway 87 North in New York laid out for us.

"I would send it your way right now, but this freaking guy had the freaking nerve to tell me that I had to put my freaking suitcase in the freaking trunk. These low life, coof Uber bastards has no direction." I sat in traffic glaring through the rearview mirror as he kicked my back in, I then thought about his mouth and attitude which was horrible. Not to mention the traffic, the distance, and the pay. To add insult to injury his little giggles just got to me. Reader enough was enough, he had become unbearable.

I pulled over on interstate highway 87 North, I popped the trunk, I opened my door, I walked to the trunk, I grabbed his suitcase and I threw it on the divider. I then walked to his door, I graciously opened it and I demanded that he get the heck out of my car.

"Huh?" He responded in shock.

"You can't just leave me here." He pleaded.

"Watch me!" I confirmed.

"Tell Mr. West to call you another Uber or bring his Tail from California to pick you up off the side of the road before your fat nasty rude behind melts!"

"Freaking low life bastard" He screamed. Meanwhile I was on my way to the next exit. And couldn't wait to tell someone about what just took place.

"You won't believe this!" I paused as I realized who I was speaking to. I looked at my Teri's picture which was set as my screen saver as I continued with the story.

"Babe you know you shouldn't have done that." She rejected all my justifications for kicking the passenger out on the highway. And she was right reader, but it was a done deal so I couldn't take it back now.

Chapter Six

"Listen babe, I was just on the phone with my Sister. She just reminded me of her wedding." A Wedding???? was all I could think of. I haven't been to a wedding since the age of being knee high to a duck. Oh well it is what it is." I continued in thought.

"So, when is the wedding?" I asked.

"This weekend" She whispered. Without any eye contact.

"You're joking?!" I said with a stern look. But her raised eyebrow screamed that she was so serious. With everything going on, not to mention the lack of money. She mustarded up this magical two days-notice trip headed to Greensboro, N.C.

Okay I thought being that I'm forced into agreement I had to act accordingly. First, we need a rental. I didn't want to add miles, wear, or tear on any of our personal cars. But how will this manifest?!

After a day or two I found a solution. "Hey Bob, I'm having what seems to be a Water pump issue." After a brief silence;

"Come on Jack you know what to do. Call Brian. He'll take care of ya. He likes ya!" In other words, reader; This one's on you, Jack!

That's what he thought. But like my boy said, I called Brian. Only I had Brian set the visit up for Friday close to closing, this way I can have the rental and keep it all weekend. It worked.

"Jack you don't need a rental do ya?" Bob asked me.

"Sure I do, Bob. I have a whole family of girls. We have to get around until that lemon of a BMW acts right!" Once again he was quiet as a church mouse.

"Okay Jack go get the darn rental!"

"I Love you to my boy!" Was my only reply.

"Yeah yeah, Jack!" He replied.

"Ok bae its 1 am, get up so we can hit the road before the traffic gets bad." Teri just smiled at me and rolled over as I attempted to get her out of the bed. My wife works like a slave. 8-12 hours daily, sometimes double shifts. She had no intentions of adhering to such a disturbance. She was the wrong person to try to get out of the bed. Especially during the wee hours of the morning. After a handful of attempts I managed to get the lady of my life to get one foot out of the bed.

Meanwhile the kids sat fully clothed impatiently waiting to leave.

"Ok babe I'm going to take a quick shower. So if there's anything that you want to handle you might as well handle it now." While waiting, I decided that I will take a couple trips so I can get a couple dollars to take with us. I logged into my Uber App and went online. The first job I got was in Highland Park, New Jersey. After cruising through this town, which is most known for its speed traps I reached my destination.

"What's up buddy?" I greeted the customer. The little Italian climbed into the BMW and became aggressive from the door.

"Listen driver we have to go pick up my friend." Not again! I thought as I looked at him while I let what he demanded register.

"Is that what you put on the App.?" I asked the little boy.

"WHAT?! Either we go get my boy or this car moves nowhere." He threatened as he used he left foot to hold the rear car door open.

"Listen buddy, I can't do that" I recanted. He was now getting comfortable in the back seat. I already felt as if I were getting chumped let alone bullied by a kid reader, so I refused to adhere to his demands. But after a minute-long mirror standoff (Stare) the little boy dug into his pocket and revealed a $10 bill. He then threw it on the front seat.

Silly me, but I decided to take him to pick his friend up. (did someone whisper money talks) I put the car in drive and made my way to the friend's house. When we arrived at his friend's house, he said his what ups and I quickly got them to their destination and out of my car.

After riding around for an hour or so I decided to check on the team. Teri's phone rang until the voicemail picked up. Typical I thought. Trying to contact this woman is like getting an interview with Oprah. I then began to dial Isha (step-daughter). The phone rang and rang and continued to ring. A bell went off in my head. I realized whose number I was calling and immediately shut that down. Isha was worse than Teri. Never answers her phone and always had an excuse for not answering the phone.

Sometimes I wonder am I the only weirdo in love that deals with these shenanigans?! I dialed my oldest step-daughter's number. I wasn't surprised to get her on the first ring.

"Yolanda is Mommy in the shower?" All I heard was crickets on the other end of the phone.

"No and I'm ready to go!" Kay kay yelled loud enough for me to hear her from the background.

"Hey Babe!" Teri answered

"Heyyy!" I replied. Are you up?" I asked the lady in my life. From the response she gave I knew that she was nowhere near ready. And for Teri to get out of the King size bed we shared I would have to put hands on her. So I decided to make my way back home.

By the time I got back to the house the Sun was beating me. Yup 5am and Teri was still under the quilt. I glanced at my woman and told the kids that I had to close the door so that I could get dressed. The whole time my mind was in the gutter. That 7-hour ride could put a strain on my manhood! (Chuckle chuckle) So I decided to do something about it before I lost the opportunity.

"Ok, is everybody packed and ready to go?!" All members of the team looked at one another to see if everyone had what they needed for the long weekend ahead of them. Kay kay stood in the doorway with a head set on her ears and cell phone in her back pocket.

"Somebody is ready to go!" I chimed.

"Been ready!" She corrected me. Kay kay was the Gangster. (Well in her young mind she was!) I then looked at the others. Then there was Yolanda (The oldest) she was all smiles of innocence) and Isha (let's nothing bother her) slowly made her way out of her what one would consider a Bat cave.

"Hey Jack a riah!" Isha chimed.

"Heyyy!" I replied. Now that everyone except Mommy was ready to walk out the door, I decided to blow the bathroom up. Being that Mommy was in there I just opened the door and walked inside. Guess who wasn't getting ready. Instead she was there to occupy the toilet! Immediately My belly began to bubble. The last thing I needed right now was this kind of situation.

"Make sure you wash your hands bae!" I joked.

"What boy! Don't play with me." She replied. I had a good laugh out of that. I love my little family. I have a woman that was a diehard fan of mines and young ladies who was treating me like the father of the year.

So in return I cherished the ground that they walked on. Each and every one of them brought something unique to the table. Kay kay and Isha prepped, and cooked, and Yolanda baked the most exclusive desserts on file.

Now it was time to hit the road. There was something missing that will be very fruitful during this journey.

"Prayer"

"Lord we thank you for this day. We pray that you will take the wheel of this vehicle and cover our family with your protection. We pray that you will allow your light to shine through us, so that we may be a blessing to others. We pray for a fun, loving, and safe trip. We thank you for your Love. In Jesus name we pray. Amen." Like her Mother, Yolanda was a praying young lady. So I knew that we were in good hands from this second forward.

We were now on the road. Destination; Greensboro, North Carolina. I pulled into a Stop and Shop which was located on the interstate Highway 27, Somerset, New Jersey. While there we went inside to get ice and a few items to drink and snack on while on the road. We grabbed cold cuts, Fruits, Juices, Waters etc. then we were off.

An hour into the trip; "Okay I'm going on a picnic I'm bringing Apples"

"I'm going on a picnic and I'm bringing Apples and Bananas" Isha followed suit. As I listened I was lost and when she screamed that it was my turn I was lost for words! But like the others I fell right in line.

"I'm going on a picnic and I'm bringing Apples, Bananas and Carrot Juice." I stuttered.

"I'M (Kay kay used Emphasis) going on a picnic and I'M bringing Apples, Bananas, Carrot Juice and DEEEZZ NUTZ!" she caught everybody off guard with that one. In a session that would had normally gotten her jumped on was over looked and brushed off as fun time.

"Keep my Kay kay in prayer, reader! The only reaction she got from everyone was chuckles and cries of laughter. From my peripheral I saw Teri give her that look that whispered;

"Tighten up little girl." I then looked in the rear-view mirror and shook my head.

"Terrible" I thought aloud.

"Hold up Isha let us hear one of your jokes." Teri was very excited to introduce the hidden talents of the girls to me that I had yet to experience.

"A Cowboy rides into town on Friday, stays for three days, then leaves on Friday. How did he do this?"

"He was dreaming" said one.

"He left Wednesday" said another.

"I got it I got it. He never had a Horse." Kay kay answered.

"No! No! No!" Isha replied.

"So what's the answer?" mommy asked.

"The Horse name was Friday! Ma." Everyone was in tears.

"Okay I have another one." She added.

"No No Isha we don't want any jokes that we can't get the answer to." Teri said to shut her down.

Yes reader this was used as an outlet to satisfy the boredom. But it didn't stop there. We had been riding for hours now it's like every other song was about what family meant to us.

"I want coffee." Was all they needed to hear. We took the next exit. The Dunkin donuts unfortunately was a self-service branch and it didn't have working Coffee dispensers. So we ended that and jumped back on the Highway 95 and headed south.

As we were exiting, there was a guy using all his muscles to push this overweight female into the back seat of a Caravan. After looking and nudging one another we all found humor in this sight.

The next exit we came to everyone got their light and sweet coffees. Well mommy was cool with her Mocha Macchiato (No sugar).

Chapter Seven

"Hey sister" Teri chimed into the voice box of her Android cellular phone.

"Don't hey me, Messy! where you at?" was her sister's immediate reply.

All I heard was "MESSY???" But OKKKK. If she likes it, I love it! Tammy was a country girl who was straight forward. My first impression was she is full of drama. But I didn't want to prejudge her. The last thing I wanted to project was an image that would make my future wife look anything other than that flawless woman I will be spending the rest of my life with. By this time, we were in the South.

"I'm 30 some odd minutes away." Teri informed her. I was deep in thought with what would become of this trip.

"Be yourself" I whispered. Of course, I wanted to be accepted by my extended family but I wasn't willing to sacrifice my integrity to get those smiles.

"Tell ya boo I said hi." She screamed thru the mouthpiece of the phone. I smiled and spoke to her.

"Hi aunt Tammmiieee!" the girls harmonized. One would be so proud of these girls. They were raised with respect, integrity, morals, and ambition to earn what they wanted out of life. And mom was their hero. She's the perfect example. She struggled and struggled. And after years of struggle she's finally reaping the benefits.

"Hey Isha!"

"Hey Kay Kay!"

"Hey Sunflower!"

"Sunflower???" I thought. I then looked around to search faces of this Sunflower character.

"That's Yolanda's nickname Jack!" Kay kay chimed. Aunt Tammy didn't have a clue that we were making our way to the street that led to the complex.

"Tammy, did you reserve the room for me and my babe?" Teri had to ask her sister about this room at least 10 times. She asked so many times that I was beginning to doubt her as well.

"Pank I done told yo tail that I reserved it. Now where y'all at?" She added. By this time, we were entering the complex. (For years reader, I've heard stories of the South. This scenic view was nothing of the sort. When a person that haven't been anywhere South besides South of New Jersey, the vision of the south is a house seated on acres of land. Maybe some farm animals grazing the grass, or dirt roads with no endings. But to see huge mall developments and condominium complexes caught me by surprise.

"We outside auntie!" Isha screamed. Before we could pull into the parking space a hand full of females came running down the two-flight staircase. Reader If you could picture the Classic

"Color Purple movie" when Nettie and Celie reunited after being separated from one another. This was the joyous scenery of Teri reconnecting with her family. There was hugs and kisses that were unstoppable. I was so happy to see my family's happiness.

While they ran into the house I became the bag man. So with me being the only man on the scene I didn't have a problem doing so. I made my way through the door with two arms full of luggage.

"This is the love of my life." Teri told her sisters and nieces. They were all genuinely excited to meet me. One of the nieces was so into her comfort zone that she began to expose a story about a car accident that she had that basically challenged her mental and emotional stability. And she didn't mind sharing the details.

"My name is Salina I'm the favorite niece and I will be the one to prepare the meal you will be eating." I wasn't used to sitting at anyone else's table but the lady in my life. Well G'mom, Bakann and of course some eatery or something will always be an exception. But to just look forward to having a stranger's hands prepare my meals was something I had to mentally prepare for.

"Oh ok, I look forward to tasting your food sweetie." I replied with a smile.

"This is my babe" Teri whispered to an elder lady. "Jack this is my mom" I thought that I saw a ghost. I've seen pictures and post of her, but to actually meet this woman was uncomfortable but an honor at the same time.

"Hey mom" after an embrace, I've heard so much about you. Her response was a smile.

After the girls were settled and everyone was acquainted it was time to get to the place me and Teri will be staying for the weekend.

"Sister I'm ready to go to the room." Tammy looked at Teri and began to make her way to the front door. They said their BE RIGHT BACKS, we climbed into the loaner. And for some reason I felt bad like I swindled my dealer or something. Anyway, we were on our way to the Clarion Hotel. Which was in Greensboro, N.C. as well.

Maybe 10 minutes of driving up a few long streets and down a highway or two we breezed through the not so busy traffic and pulled into one of the two Hotels that sat off to side of the highway.

We pulled into the front lobby and while Teri and Tammy went inside to pay for the room I kept the car running as if they were going inside to stick up a bank and I was the getaway car.

Meanwhile this brother came up to the car extended his hand and with a bright smile, He asked;

"You want to go get some drinks, smokes or some type of intoxicants?" I looked at him and with a sincere smile, I declined.

10 minutes' tops they were walking out with key-card in hand. "We're in room 240 babe." Teri chimed.

"Oh I'm sorry babe, that's Dan. Tammy's man"

"Yeah son been trying to get me high since y'all left." I replied. The only intoxicant I need is the pillow that will be snuggling my head. I was ready to find the closest wherever and just sleep the rest of the weekend away.

Of course, this was only a thought reader. We each grabbed a hand full of bags and swiped the card to the side door.

"Daaang, Jamaicans must live in this joint" I thought aloud as the midst of marijuana hit my nose.

"Yeah and I'm about to go door to door until I find the supplier and demand mines." Dan wanted in, and he wasn't haven't it no other way. I looked at my sister-in-law and couldn't vision her in nobody's weed cloud. So I figured she was the conditional tolerant type. Dan on the other hand was 0-60. He was more like the what one would consider a functional addict. Kept drugs in his system but kept a job to supply his habit. We continued to the room that will be housing us for the next few days.

As I walked through the door it kicked in that I was almost 1000 miles from home. This was the furthest I've ever been from the City of New Brunswick. I felt so far away from home. As I was getting home sick I received a phone call.

"Peace Hog?" I listened as my cousin as he got in an emotional ventilation mode. Cuz whatever you do, don't challenge them pigs out there. Them bastards are totally different than back home. Remember you have to make it back home. And let them Bama Hittas talk."

"It's just a visit so you need to make it back home." That call was followed by a call from mom.

"Hey Son Son! I pray that you and Miss Teri "My daughter" make it there safely." I listened to my Bakann. And was becoming content with my current situation. I was even more happy to be on the phone than usual. The call made me feel more at home than afar.

"Hey mom!!!" Teri was genuinely attached to my mother as my mother was to her. This was almost shocking to me. I'm so used to hearing: NO I DON'T WANT TO MEET NOBODY! Versus I COOKED, WHEN YALL COMING OVER? They shared a brief chat and disconnected. The calls didn't stop there though. Mook gangster and Q Block Away checked in. Mook said if I needed him he was on the first thing smoking.

"700 miles away. But OK!" Was my thoughts.

Teri got an extra bed in case the girls felt the need to be with us instead of their family. Even the closest family can sometimes make family feel like a visitor. And with this information Teri always make room for the girls.

Together Teri and I began to unpack. Well I unpacked as Teri undressed for a shower. It was then she informed me about the rehearsal for the big day. So I dragged my feet as I followed suit. I was so exhausted, the last thing I expected was to be leaving the room for anything but smoking a Newport.

Moments later she returned with a towel wrapped around her dripping wet body.

"Babe you need to get ready. I don't want to have Sissy waiting." After fingering through the duffle bag I pulled my Buffalo jeans out and shirt to match. I slipped them on and became one with the mirror. Although I was my own biggest critic. No matter what the outside looked like my insides told me that I still had it. So this took a few minutes with a little help from the lady in my life confirming with me that I still had what it takes to walk and talk like that guy!

"Babe you are so sexy!" Everything she said to me began and ended with an ego stroke and smile. I could be the angriest guy on the Planet until I caught eye contact with this woman. It was then that nothing else mattered. With that I quickly got fresh to deaf and fly as ever. Teri had no problem matching my Fly! She slipped on her thigh high mini skirt, that I thought revealed too much thigh. But her full figure wore it. And wore it well!

"Were leaving out now Tammy." She then smiled as I held the door open for her to make her way through. (Yes reader Chivalry still lives.) I was raised to respect women and Children. I speak first! I smile! I will Yes Ma'am/Sir you! Thank you! And Please you of course. Bakann did a good job on this one.

Chapter Eight

After a 10-15 min drive we pulled up to a church on a hill surrounded by a parking lot that could be seen from a highway.

We parked and said our Hellos and as we were making our way to the front door, I ran back to the car to add fire to my Newport. After a few pulls I realized that I really wasn't too into the cigarettes. I dudded the half out and stuck the remainder back into the cigarette box.

Now inside I looked around at the unfamiliar faces and smiled with each greeting.

"This is Such and such!"

"This is my babe; such and such." Just to name a few.

"Come here babe" Teri now had me by the hand and was escorting me to a smaller guy.

"Hey Uncle George!!!!!!!! Teri was very excited for me to meet Uncle George. He was like a second father to her and it meant everything to her to let him know that as she likes to put it that she has finally found the man of her dreams.

"Hey baby" He responded. And this guy here is Jack, right?"

"Uncle George she says with the biggest smile on her face Yes, this is My love, My everything, My Jack Hoagalino." Yes reader, she said my entire name with so much pride.

"Babe this is my uncle George. My Uncle George has given me the blueprint of how a man is supposed to treat me since I was a little girl."

"Hey Uncle George" I spoke. Uncle George struck me as that one person that was loved by everyone. He's also that family member that ran from the BS as fast as he could.

"Yes Uncle George, this right here is the love of my life. My man of God."

"Uncle George I love this man so much!" Uncle George had an ear to ear smile across his face while Teri spoke great things about me.

"Uncle George, he's the one!!!! Uncle George he exceeds everything you've ever told me to expect out of a man." Uncle George's Kool aid smile confirmed that he was convinced that she had finally found the right one.

"Jack its very nice to meet you!" Uncle George then began to drop some words of wisdom concerning Teri's and I relationship.

"I just want you to know that it's important to keep God first." He proceeded. That's what will make a successful union. Also, she is to serve you and vice versa; you are to serve her the same." So genuine, this guy was. From start to finish he gave good information.

It felt good reader. Especially, to hear pointers from the guy that raised Teri. Although Teri and I had already been practicing a so close to God relationship there was always room for improvement. And keeping God first, is something that was established from the beginning. They both knew that this was so necessary. So, to hear this same attribute from the one that taught her who-what-why the man in her life should be was a direct connection for him.

"Thank you" was all I could mustard up. The hug, the smile and shake only solidified this meeting. Although there weren't too many places to disappear Uncle George and his jolly wife vanished in midair. After meeting cousin so and so, auntie Ice cream, nephew Peanut butter, I needed a breath of fresh air. So I walked outside to pull on a Newport from my pack of cigarettes.

"What's good Hitta!" I looked at 20 cent worth of meat on the bones of this wanna be gangster and almost laughed in his face. Not you, I almost thought aloud.

"What up tho!" I replied instead.

"What up wit you Hitta!" the perpetrator countered. He was so aggressive that he almost fooled me to believe that he was somebody's Triple OG. Or Big Homie of the South. But with me being stuck in the worst parts of the Penile, (The Great Northern State, East Jersey State, New Jersey State Prisons) wrestling with the best of them, I thought Jack we've been in this situation on more than one occasion. If not worse. So it was like brushing teeth.

"I'm coolin." I told him.

"What bring yo Tail down these parts of the Woods Hitta?!" this stranger asked. I tried to tune him out, but he was so persistent that I had to respond. With one eye shooting for the stars and the other hanging to the left, This bag of bones was zeroed in like a hungry eagle.

"That's Teri's man crazy. You need to sit yo Tail down somewhere, Lil moe." Whoever the female was that came to my aid wasn't much help.

"Listen here Hitta, I'm Teri family. If you hurt her I'm a whip dat Tail!" Reader, It took everything in me for me not to knock all three of his teeth down his throat.

"You hear me Hitta?" He continued.

"Shoot Hitta, I done been shot." That left his lips like a Gorilla's growl.

"I know you think I'm jiving, Look Hitta." He was now pulling the pant leg to his 3 sizes too big shorts over the knee to show me that he was grazed.

"Yeah the fool that shot me Hitta, walking round with a groin bag for the rest of his life" Clearly this intimidation tactic was Lil moe way of climbing out of his shell of inferiority to such a superior breed of Hitta.

No I didn't feel threatened by none of what he said. In fact I thought he was kind of funny. The last thing I wanted was to have my Lady's sister wedding sabotaged because of an ignorant family member. But I couldn't bite my tongue any longer.

"Listen lil Hitta, I done been shot too Hitta!" I told him. The Hitta that shot me disappeared." Lil moe eyes became big as fish. But it didn't stop there. I was now ready to see if he was really bout that life his lips claim he was living.

"On another note, I disrespect ya family on the regular. Forget Teri!" I continued to provoke him with; I told that bird if she step outta line while we down here I will punish her tail and leave her tail right here with you Country Hittas!"

"So I think I'm ready for that whoopin you was yappin bout." Lil moe was now all smiles of innocence.

"Man Forget all that Hitta, you Gangster! Teri know her Mickey Fickey place. Hell, If she getz that tail whooped she deserves that tail whoop." After seeing the mutt come out of this killer I figured he was all mouth. Reader, although there was nothing soft about me, I was far from a bully so I gave him my famous chuckle and was back inside.

......REHEARSAL.....

"Okay I need everyone to pair with someone." Spat the lady who was walking around with a clip board in hand. She was the one that will be to orchestrating everything that was about to take place. As the participants stood she began to pair each of them with a matching pair that would complement the other.

Isha who was so uncomfortable with the chubby guy, just rolled with the punches, She was good at camouflaging things so it wouldn't show either way. Yolanda was all smiles. I could tell that she was a little uncomfortable as well, it was all fun time for Kay kay. Teri on the other hand was happy for her sister's big day so it was show time even if she had to walk with Kermit himself. She did her thing so well one would think that she was rehearsing for her big day.

Everyone was paired and lined up to march into as Maid of Honor, Bribe's maids, Flower girls, Ring bearers so on and so forth.

Meanwhile there was another little guy (photographer) running around trying his best to get the best shots that he could gather with what little height he had.

"Go back out again." The young lady whispered as the music came to a halt.

After countless attempts the cast finally got to hit it off. I sat back with a good eye on everything moving. One of my eyes were on the Culprit (Lil moe) who ran around like some body's runner. Every few seconds he had his hand extended for someone to recognize that he was in the building.

"Okay everyone can help themselves." Sis was her own host for the most part. I found a seat and relaxed as Teri made her way to the line of snacks and refreshments. Cheese, crackers, juices, water, exotic drinks and hors d'oeuvres. Everyone was dressed down as if it were a dress down Friday at work. The groom walked around with a bright smile across his face. He was so happy to become Savannah's husband.

"So babe, sissy is having a Bachelorette party."

"Oh okay" I replied. After a long pause, and the sound of crickets Teri continued with; "But I don't think that I'm going to attend." I just listened to what she had to say. When she completed her indirect question of Permission, I asked;

"Okay, so where's the Bachelor party?"

"Huh?!" was her response. Sissy and the girls are having a nice intimate dinner." She added. One thing that I never understood reader, was the reaction that the other party displayed when it came to the acceptance of the same things that they brought to the table.

Of course I wanted to go to the Bachelor party! What guy wouldn't?! Especially if my lady is attending the Bachelorette party! Women have a problem with trusting the man to do the same things that they feel they are strong enough to do themselves. Such as attending a Bachelorette party. Oh well Moving right along!!!

"Ask Jerome." She finally spat.

As she made her way back to her sisters I found Jerome.

"So Brah, what's up with the Bachelor party?" I chimed. Jerome shrugged his shoulders and with a smile he whispered that he wanted to go Bowling.

"Bowling?!" Did this Hitta just say that he'd rather Bowl as an alternative. Yes reader while his wife Turnt up at an undisclosed location to attend a Bachelorette Party! The groom will be sweating bullets on someone's bowling alley. (Oh well if he likes it I love it!) I almost thought aloud. But then it hit me that he loved her enough to trust that she would act according and decided to give her space on her special day.

After the Cheese and crackers appetizers everyone packed their personals and was told this time tomorrow to meet at the church where the bride and groom will be tying the knot. So everyone one but the Groom found the exit. Some had transportation, others were transported and there were a few that took the highway exit. Wherever that lead to.

Back at the room Teri has a phone call with Sis. about how they didn't really want to attend the Bachelorette party. But they were all prepping for the Outing. Teri went and dug out her best threads and was immediately out the door.

I decided that I will stay in the room while she attended the bachelorette party. An hour of being separated after being inseparable for months now I realized that I was missing my baby. I jumped in the shower and as soon as I dried off someone was tapping at the door.

"Yo" I answered.

"Yo Terrell there?" Is the words that were whispered through the door. I immediately glanced at the clock (which read 2am), and all I could think of was: "Who is this at my door!"

"Yo money you got the wrong door." The Hitta must've got the picture, because his response was;

"My bad". 10 years prior to this night the Police, the National guards, the Fire dept. etc would have all been summoned, because my thoughts would have headed left and anything in my way would've been a target. Sometimes Hittas are sneakier than females! And the females make it so easy that it builds the confidence of the guys to overstep their boundaries. But whatever.

(An hour later guess who walks thru the door reader?)

"Hi babe you hungry? I bought you some Wendy's?" I turned over and without brushing my teeth or anything I took hold of the bag, reached into grab the 4 for 4 meal and as I half unwrapped the Jr. Bacon cheeseburger I took a monster bite. That was chased down with a Big gulp (Hi-C drink.)

Meanwhile Teri found the bathroom to freshen up a bit. I anxiously awaited her return. I have been starving for them gutz, but that alone time was not available.

Well reader, tonight was the night that I will be getting fed.

"Look at my baby." I almost thought aloud. Clearly she had similar thoughts racing thru her head because she was all smiles of guilt. With the towel covering half of her full figure she strutted her woman stuff towards me with the look of lust screaming through the pupils of her wanting eyes. I slowly pulled the cover revealing a fully charged battery pack. Teri eyes instantly grew wide. Not to mention the wet lips that her glistening tongue refused to halt from wetting.

"C'mere you." I whispered. I didn't have to repeat myself. She was already in route. The scent of her body spoke soft volumes of pleasure. There was only one mission and these two were the only key players that could make this meeting come to life.

Once the bed became filled with these two and the desires that they craved, it's almost as if they were in competition to see who will be responsible for the other's pleasure. They touched, they tasted, they spoke naughty whispers and their bodies conversation spoke;

"Everything is a go." That much-needed alone time took them exactly where they need to be.

Well today was the big day and like Teri, I was looking forward to what lied ahead. The clothes that we will be wearing were pressed and laid across the additional bed that was in the room.

"Okay babe we have very little time. I need you to pick my sister up from the hotel and bring her to the house." I felt as if I were at work on my vacation. So I was hesitant about picking her sister up, but once again I didn't want to make Teri look bad while on the trip.

"What's the address sweetie?" I should've retracted the sweetie.

"Sweetie, Babe?!" Was her response in question. One thing she had a problem with was being called sweetie. I had a habit of calling every one sweetie. Sweetie to me was just a figure of speech, so I used it with endearment. Unless I ran across a Hitta that thought they were tough. And just to get up under his skin, I would sometimes sweetie them as well. This was used as a method to provoke them. And Teri knew this so she normally cleared herself from this as a whole.

"I'm sorry!" I recanted.

"Whatever" was her immediate response. But thank you!" She added. That was said with a smile.

"Oh yeah?!" I replied. Thank you was another innuendo. THANK YOU was sometimes used as another way to say "Forget You!"

Of course this isn't one of those times but one reaction deserves another. So I accepted the Thank You. Anyway, I went to get her sister who was occupied with two nieces.

"Uncle can we stop by the market?" I quickly took them there. That stop at the supermarket was at a gas station on one of the main highways that sold everything; from Cigarettes, to Alcohol, there were even T-shirts and Soul food. From there we were taken to the church then to the house where the others were.

"Hey Jack" Spoke Uncle George.

"Hey Uncle George."

"How you doing brother?" He greeted then once again began to give me the Dos and Don'ts. As if he left something out the first hour therapy session we had. Typical Uncle stuff!!! So I took it.

Never make your woman feel like she's not doing something right! Like she's not doing enough. Remember that you two are a team! No one is bigger than the other! Yes, she has to respect what you say and you do as such, but this goes both ways!" So on and so forth. Overall Uncle George was a cool guy. And towered over his little frame was the wife who stood by his side filled with all smiles and had just as much if not more to add onto what he had already shared.

"Thank you Thank you and Thank you!" I told them both. I think we will be ok." I then made a detour in the opposite direction from this guy.

Chapter Nine

The setting was the setting of something one would catch on television.
Something scripted by a famous writer of a most sought out screen play.

The first person seen after the doorman was the dipped in black groom, who patiently waited for his wife. Soft gospel music whispered by: Chrisette Michele as the maid of honor took her place followed by the flower girls who the bride's maids trailed. One thing that stuck out was how uncomfortable was how Isha seemed to be drug by the guy on her arm who was three times her little size. Then there was the ring boy who dragged his feet.

Everyone in the audience stood attentive. Some had tears flooding their eyes, others had their I-Phones, Galaxy's, I-Pads. Or some sort of camera in the air with intentions of catching the best moment that they can. Finally, the bride entered through the hand-held doors chauffeured by none other than Uncle George. She brought with her a tear-filled face with an innocent smile stretching her cheeks. So, Beautiful she was...

For a second I envisioned my Teri walking down the aisle to me as I stood impatiently waiting for her arrival. But I figured that on Divine timing! And that our time will soon come. So I had to stay focused and step out of my own selfish thoughts.

Never been to a Wedding where the bride and groom was blessed by multiple Pastors. I mean one after the other they took their precious time to Touch and agree with them both. Jerome had a soft cry as they were communed.

And then it happens.....

"Dear family and friends, we are gathered here today in the sight of God and in the presence of these witnesses, to join this man Jerome Hinton and this woman Savannah Wells in Holy Matrimony. Which is an honorable estate, instituted by God to fulfill us as individuals and as a couple, and to conform us, as maturing believers, into the image of Christ."

"Jerome and Savannah have chosen to be married in the Lord's house as a testimony of their faith in God and as a witness to all present that they desire to honor their Lord and Savior in their lives and in their home. May our heavenly Father look down upon this event with His favor.

May the Lord Jesus Christ be present and add His blessing. May the Holy Spirit attend and seal these vows in love."

After the communion was the Reception. The Reception was located at a place that seemed to be up in the mountains. Deep in the mountains maybe a town away. When we got to the dim lite fluorescent lights flashing throughout the entire hall There were family and friends catering three tables. Not to mention the five-story wedding cake that towered over 90% of the participants.

Maybe my mind was playing tricks on me but it appears that the reception was more packed than the wedding.

As Teri sat at the King Arthur table with the bride the groom and his family I stood by the door dumbfoundedly until Kay kay directed me to come to the table where she and Salina had set aside for the two of them along with a few others.

While there I sat, and chuckled as Salina clowned everyone. Including the food. She expressed how bland the flavor was and that this food couldn't touch hers. I found it comical. Well she was a natural comedian herself. So I found it hard, Extremely hard to take her serious.

"Look at Moe. A Darn nutt case!" She chimed.

"Jack tell my cousin what Lil moe said to you" I just looked at Kay kay. Only because that was supposed to be an inside joke. I didn't want everyone to know that I had a beef with a family member already. It hasn't been 48 hours yet! But being that the cat was out of the bag I figured Oh well I'll let her know the clown stuff he did.

"He's a straight punk!" Salina confirmed what I already knew. She was straight up and down.

"Uncle I know my cousin. And Lil moe is a straight up punk!" This time she said that with feeling.

"Come on baby cakes!" Teri was now pulling my hand and escorting me to the dance floor. The dance floor was occupied with maybe 50 people who were entertaining the Electric slide, the Wobble baby and the Cha Cha Cha!

"Is he recording us babe?" She asked.

"Yes" I told my wife as the cameraman aimed the camera at us and blinded my eyes for the next 5 minutes.

"Oh well show time!" I thought as I began to Cha Cha and Electrically slide across the floor.

While we danced, the girls came with a guy on their arm. "This is our Uncle Terrell." Yolanda chimed.

"Your brother!" Kay kay chimed. I smiled as I extended my hand. He returned the greeting.

"Okay y'all, everyone line up for cake." Savannah yelled over the music. The line became so long so fast!

"Hold up, did Lil moe just walk to the front of the line" Salina thought aloud. She had no problem with who heard what either.

"The whole family was gangster, huh!" I thought.

"Okay ladies get ready to catch the bouquet." Savannah chimed. Everyone stood behind the bride and the person least expected to catch the bouquet was the person to catch it.

"Move Kay kay" Teri yelled. Kay kay just kept walking with a smile across her face with the bundle of flowers in hand.

After everyone walked away she whispered; that she caught the bouquet for mommy. Everyone lined up for cake. With cake in hand and such an awesome wedding experience, it was time to find the exit.

"Thank you babe, You can't imagine what this experience has done for me and our family. Not only did you get to meet the family but at the most vulnerable time of my life you are herrrreee!!!"

"God is definitely moving!" She added.

Like most women, Teri was more Bi-polar than a pregnant female. One minute she was the happiest go lucky girl on the block, the next she would be kicking and screaming about the things that were not in order. But when she was excited about the Goodness of God, that excitement had the tendency to go from 0-100 in a matter of seconds.

We went to her sister's house first, then made our rounds to say our good byes. Of course no one wanted to see us go. No one ever does! But like everyone else we had a whole other life and life styles to tend to.

So for the next 500 miles or 7-8 hours (layman's terms) we ended this and made plans for the next trip. Kay kay and Teri were able to stay up with me and helped keep me alert by sharing songs and exchanging a joke or two followed by riddles.

As I continued to eat the highways and the byways I began to think of how I just ended up in Greensboro NC. How we just up and with very little money traveled miles away. I thought about the experience I've just had. How I dealt with more than one situation head on! There was a Shift taking place in my life. And I kind of like it.

Chapter Ten

"Home sweet home!" I whispered. Everyone jumped out of the car and as they all fought to get to the bathroom I grabbed as many bags as I could.

After unpacking the car and filling the Living room with the bags, without warning I tried to sneak out of the house.

"Babe where are you going?" Teri asked. One would say after such a long and exhausting weekend everything would be blocked out for rest.

"I have to turn this Uber on Sweetheart." I told her.

"No babe. My man just drove all the way from North Carolina he's getting some rest." She spoke to me as if she were speaking to herself in third person.

"Okay dear" I confirmed. But as soon as I heard that light snore creep out of her nose I was shutting the front door to our home behind me.

"Hey what's up youngen?!" I greeted the young African American kid.

"How you doing Sir" Was his immediate response. Very respectful, this kid was. Clearly, he was raised right. Whether Velvet glove or Iron fist! Whatever his parents/guardian method was it showed in his demeanor.

"That's a nice house you live in."

"Thanks a lot. My parents had to bust their behinds by working two three jobs to make this life for us." After a brief pause; It's a Gift and Curse." He added.

"A Gift and a Curse?!" I questioned.

"Yes Sir, being able to live here the 16 years that I've been here with everything that living here gives me and my family. The maid, the butler, the home schooling, the catering service etc. But the curse is the fact that like my parents, I must work my behind off for the rest of my life to keep it."

"Wow, this is mind blowing!" I thought. The thought process of this boy. Most kids these days thought process is MY PARENTS HAVE THIS AND THAT SO I HAVE! WHY WORK FOR IT?!"

"Yes Sir, so please don't think for one second that this is my reality! The kid whispered. "My goal is to get into Business School, graduate with a Business management degree and be able to run my parents Business so that they can finally rest."

Reader, I was lost for words. But one thing that I learned from this experience is, the excuses I used to make for my children; (My children are just children so excuse them for thinking like children!) Now goes out the window. Thanks to this 16-year-old independent thinker.

"Josh, I wanna thank you for being a blessing to me." I whispered.

"You are welcome Sir. And good luck on your Dreams." He replied. Work hard to make sure that they become reality!" I felt so inspired by this goal driven intelligent kid. Might I add he looked like me.

Like each time I'm moved by something motivating or inspiring, I immediately called my wife to share with her the mark this kid made on my life.

"Well babe, you have to remember your Calling and as long as you continue to serve God He will continue to amaze you." My wife always had confirmation to the things that these people brought to the table.

"Thank you sweetheart." I showed gratitude.

"Have you been studying for your test?" Funny that she asked because since we've come back from North Carolina I've become laxed. Haven't been doing much of anything. Not to mention opening anybody's You-tube to watch a video guide for a Commercial driver's license. Last thing on my mind Reader!

"No sweetheart but I'll call to see if Pedro has anything open for us." Yup Team us! Is the only way we see things. If it's my goal, then it's her goal! In other words, we both have a test to pass.

"Pedro, I think I'm ready for that test!"

Okay friend, did you pay the financial part?" He replied.

"Yes I did." I informed him.

"Okay I have a spot for you on Thursday." He confirmed.

"Thursday?! Two days Thursday?!" I questioned. Oh well be careful what you ask for reader. You just may get it. My God is awesome. He's definitely moving!

Chapter Eleven

"How you feel babe?"

"I feel confident sweetheart." I didn't know what to feel, reader. How to feel! The truth is; I felt as if I needed more time to study. The truth is I didn't want to be embarrassed for yet another failure. The truth is I wanted to have someone take the test for me. But my Teri made it all go away when she grabbed my hands and began to speak to our God.

"Lord this is your Daughter and your Son here in your presence asking for a miracle today. You know what we need Lord. So if it's your Will Lord Jesus, we ask that you make this possible and add this addition to our family."

"Yes Lord, we thank you in advance" I quietly added to her Prayer. For the next two hours, I studied like never before. Then it happened.

"Jack it's your turn." Chimed Kevin (Driving instructor) As I made my way to the Box truck, the chills from fear immediately began to seep in.

"Come on ma Hitta, we got this." I told the fear. But to no avail I had the fear of God in me.

"Good morning Sir, how are you." As he began to read off the instructions and conduct of how he wanted me to inspect the truck everything blanked out. But when I started my inspection things began to come back to me.

I began with a Safe start. Aced it, then there was the Air brake test. Aced it. In cab inspection, Aced it. Now it was time to go under that hood. Mind you reader, I'm far from a mechanic. Shoot, I can't even put a wall unit together. Let alone someone's engine. But I went in because that's what I came to do. After seven times of failing the written test one would think that this part would be smooth sailing. Sad to say that I failed once again. But this time I realized what my mistake was.

Whenever a person take an inspection class the instructor records the inspection on the truck or vehicle that that person that's being prepared to take the test will be using. But my mistake was watching and studying the You-tube videos instead of the recording that my instructor had laid out for me himself.

So this is one to grow on. Study the recording that your instructor records for you as he walks you through the session. I learned from this and made plans to Aced the next one. But now I would have to wait until I get extra money to invest in another test. Oh well it's only 3-$400 away.

I thanked him for the opportunity and the time that he gave me. When I informed my Teri who was smiling ear to ear, She immediately began to praise God and continued to smile.

"Babe, I know this is the last thing that you want to hear, but God just told me that you weren't ready for this big jump. So you need more practice." I listened to Teri and thanked her for being who she was to me.

Chapter Twelve

"Bob I need another car." Not only did my Teri need her own means of transportation, but she earned her independence and deserved her own. So I decided that I would make that happen for her.

Like the BMW that was recently totaled Bob had another. "I think she'll like this one here Bob" I chimed as I pointed to the Black 3 series German car that stood out. This sweetie was definitely in a class by itself.

"Jack I need a down payment of at least $3 grand." This was always his method. Shoot for the greater, probably the greatest number that he could get out of his mouth. But because he respected the game we always met somewhere in the middle.

"Listen Bob, I have $1000 for you."

"Okay Jack, but you have 30 days to get the rest to me." As I was leaving out the door;

"And where's my darn book?" This was his term of endearment. Because Bob knew that I was a hood famous writer he sent questions like this as a means of acknowledging and embracing who I was to him and how much he appreciated our friendship, well business for that matter.

"When I order some more copies I'll be sure to get one to you." I assured him. After leaving the office I immediately called my Teri.

"No you didn't babe!" Was her immediate response. But for some reason she wanted the Lexus instead. So I let her keep the Lexus and the Beamer was mines. She whispered that I was a Beamer type of guy and that I looked good in it.

One would probably say with no money why live such a profound lifestyle? Or even how? My answer would probably be to become a part of the Elite. Sometimes you'd have to step out on faith alone and live like one. So I found myself leading the life of a Celebrity with no money. Some call it balling on a budget! Funny…On any given Monday you may catch me at your local Unique's thrift store.

"Church tonight babe" I always found every excuse not to go to the house of God. Sometimes I felt like a hypocrite. You know go to Church to please someone else. But tonight I was energetic to be in the house of the Lord. Maybe it was the new car that I wanted to show off! Or the blazer that I picked up from Unique's. Whatever the case was Teri and myself was there front and center for all to see.

I sat back and listened to the introduction of the speaker for the night. The dark skin guy wearing the dark shades and the tailored Black suit stepped to the Pulpit was energized from the gate;

"You brother!" He whispered as he made his way down the aisle; The Holy Spirit just told me to tell you that there is about to be a Shift in your life. God is about to give you your life back!" He then used two fingers to tap me back into the seat. I sat there with tears flowing down my face.

He told a young lady; "God was just testing you and He said to tell you that you have passed the test. When you thought you needed what your heart desired you weren't ready for it. But He's about to shower you with more than you ever desired." The young lady began to Shout and Praise dance for the next twenty minutes.

This guy I later learned was a Prophet that spoke things into existence things that a person could have only shared with God Himself. Many people were blessed this night. Even my Pastor, Pastor Bellamy of the Church who he told must make some changes involving the removal of ones that held titles in the Church. Scary but if God says, she must adhere to this.

Chapter Thirteen

While playing taxi in the streets of Plainfield, New Jersey, I picked this brother up that I figured was a comedian.

"Where you from?" He asked.

"New Brunswick" I told him. This was a town maybe 10-15 minutes away from him.

"Oh you from New Brunswick? Then you know my cousin!" He chimed. Cousin? I thought.

"Who's your cousin?" I asked him.

"Rhan'Heen" Was his immediate response. Not to mention how energetic he was with this response.

"I heard of Rhan'Heen" I told him. My Insides were so tickled reader. Like every time I meet one of Rhan'Heen's make believe family members. Especially with my mom being Rhan'Heen's mom biological sister.

"Yeah we just came back from tour. We were in London shooting the Struggle Love video." For the next 15 minutes I listened to the B.S. and let my insides be entertained by this nonsense. When he said that next week he should have back stage passes, I was done. This guy was definitely a Special need, dependent.

As he got out of the car to his destination I told him to tell his family that Jack Hoagalino said what up and that I'm a big fan of his. CREEP! Was all I could mustard up in thought.

Next customer…

As I drive 287 South I ride pass a van with bill board plastered on the side with a picture of none other than Mr. Perry himself. My confidence immediately shot to the ceiling. I began to vision myself stepping into his studio. Or maybe on the front lawn of his Estate. How will he respond to such arrogance?!

"Mr. Perry some weirdo is on the lawn demanding to see you."

Will his response be "Let him in. or Somebody call the cops!" I'm laughing right now as I slowly pass the bill board. Out of the rearview mirror I see this car jumping in and out of traffic. I didn't pay the driver much attention.

While sitting at the light impatiently waiting for it to change. I noticed this clown behind me. With his eyes not focused on the road.

"This Mother Father is about to hit me." I thought aloud. As I was thinking; "BOOM!" Was the next sound that I heard. Followed by a THUMP.

As I pull over to confront the driver and start to climbed out the car he peddle to the metal speeds off. At first I was in shock. But when it set in that he was fleeing the scene I ran back to my car and began to pursue him.

With a 0-100 in seconds BMW, needless to say I caught up to him and with the window down I yelled;

"You hit my car" But to no avail he kept going. After the blatant disrespect of "Forget Your Car!" Once more I chased him but this time I had the police on the phone.

"Listen money, I have the Police on the phone." I told him.

"Man, Forget the Cops!" He screamed.

"Sir, did you get a description of the other driver?" The police asked.

"Yo money" I yelled. The whole time I had the camera to my I Phone aimed at him. When he turned around with an extended middle finger I pushed the button to take a picture.

"Say cheese!" I thought. SNAP! SNAP!

"I got em now." I informed the Police.

"Mother Father!" He screamed as he continued to flee. Once again, I caught up to this guy and screamed that I had a full tank of gas.

"You might as well give me your address. Because wherever you go I'm coming." He laughed and pulled over. Then sat on a side street with his doors locked.

When the Police finally made it to the location he was questioned about the flee.

"I'm sorry Sir, but I'm from Britain and I'm new in the States. I wasn't sure if I were supposed to stop or keep moving to my destination." He lied.

"What in Hell!" Was all that I could mustard up.

"I must say that's the best I've heard yet!" The Police said through a chuckle. Clearly the guy that fled the scene wasn't the only one that took this Cat and Mouse chase for a game, because he was let go without a ticket or anything. I quickly got pictures of his credentials and the damages in case I never saw this guy again.

After the Police left I called my insurance company. Little did he know State farm was on deck. They live to please.

In two days, I was compensated for the damages.

Chapter Fourteen

"Bae I think that we should practice celibacy." I looked at my lady as if she was speaking another language.

"That Darn Prophet play too much!" I joked in thought.

"Okay sweetheart if it will bring out the best of us then I'm cool with it." The first night was kind of challenging. But after we got through that night it became a little less strenuous.

The second night was a little touchy feely. You know like, a brush of body parts and thangs. But we managed to get through that as well.

We figured that if we kept ourselves busy we would eventually get pass the temptations. So we got a membership at Planet fitness. I began with my Callisthenic regimen. And she took off on the treadmill. I love how energetic Teri was about the gym. She always had a drive to look good. During the day she would have little notes written on the chalkboard with quotes like;

"Lose weight Feel Great!"

"Eating well is a form of Self-respect!!!"

"Teri Don't quit!"

"God had equipped you with everything that you need to endure and win!" so on and so forth. Next to God she was her Greatest strength as a motivator. Well until I came into her life that is. Shut up reader.

Anyway, the gym was what it was. We showed up! Showed out! And bragged about our results on The Book! Good results too, y'all. After a hard workout and an argument about something, neither of the two of us can say we remember. We were both rushing to the bathroom to shower. She claims that because I always leave a ring around the tub and in return I fuss about how long she takes in the shower.

So neither of the two wanted to wait our turns. Anyway, as we both met at the shower forcing the other out of the way our sticky wet bodies mashed into each other. The last words whispered were;

"You Cheated!" There goes the so-called commitment to Celibacy. Oh well I liked it better like this anyway. And My Teri sensitivity sure didn't complain.

"Babe we can't keep doing this." I was lost for words, reader. We've just had a record breaking trip to Heaven. And she blurts out we can't keep doing this.

"I want to live right by God." She whispered.

"But I thought that we were living right by God sweetheart." I'm in my head thinking about the things that are falling into place and how we are grinding so hard to achieve them.

"Fornication is a sin in the eye sight of God. And He's definitely not pleased by our acts." She added. After having this conversation and having it confirmed with our Soul provider we felt guilty of disappointing God with such negligence. So she said no more sex until marriage. And had me pinkie swear that I wouldn't provoke her to have sex. I agreed that this time it wasn't until we were married. What she didn't know was her ring has been on lay away for Months now. I was just waiting to get the rest of the money to pay it off.

One would think that my adherence to how my Lady felt was an act of bowing down to marriage, because of my desire for sex. But the truth is right before my eyes, like the prophet whispered, there was a Shift taking place in my life and with all the blessing that we've been receiving as a team, for the first time in my life I sincerely didn't want to displease the Man that has been covering my life.

Chapter Fifteen

"Kay kay do you know mommy ring size?" I asked my step daughter.

In ten minutes or less she was in my inbox with mommy's ring finger. Reader, If you recall me informing you of who Kay kay was; you will not be surprised that she got that ring size asap. My Kay kay is the Go To of the family.

I immediately raced to Jersey Garden Mall to get her ring off lay away. When I returned, mommy had an attitude about the dishes rising to the ceiling. The girls just let her vent because they were all conspiring with my next move. So she was thrown so far off guard.

The girls suggested that we tape the next move to have a sentimental memory. So I gave Yolanda my cell phone and asked her to press record. She did. Then it happened.

I found my Teri and with her hand inside of the palm of mines, I dropped to one knee. She began to cheese and cheese and cheese some more.

"Action y'all!" after a deep breath, "It's time to take this thing to another level y'all. She deserved it." I added.

"What y'all think?" as she held her face in awe. I continued.

"Are you ready to make me the happiest man in the World?"

"Yes baby." She answered. It was then, that I began to run my mouth. A token of my appreciation! Life time journey! Y'all know the story. But yeah, this ring here is a token of who this woman here is to me. Who I trust that she will be to me for the duration of our lives! The rewards are great y'all. It only gets better." And no reader, she never saw this coming.

Even with the proposal catching her off guard at home, My Teri was Beautiful as ever. And although the kids were clowning us they were just as happy if not more.

Yes this was a big step reader. But with the unexpected things that has been taking place in our life. There was a shift taking place. Not to mention the blessings that has been assigned to our Favor, we have been leaping out on faith all year. And I'm not ashamed to scream that he's not finish.

As the kids would say; Facebook was lit all week. Almost 500 LIKES screamed across our timeline. Then the reaction that we got on Sunday at Church service was amazing.

Teri has become a celebrity overnight. At work, supermarkets, voter's registration lines etc. since becoming the future Mrs. Hoagalino.

Chapter Sixteen

After making the needed phone calls to prep for this big day, we found ourselves at the Municipal building in Somerset County.

"We're here to get a marriage license." Behind the desk was a nice Caucasian lady that had no problem helping us.

"Oh congratulations!!! I can assist you with that. I will just need a few documents. Before she named the documents she needed, Teri and I began to dig for the 6 points that are normally required at the Dmv. One can never go wrong with: Driver's license, Birth certificate, Social Security card, Proof of address etc.

"Oh you guys are prepared. I will need you to fill this paperwork out and a $25.00 money order to go along with this."

"I'm sorry, do you have a witness?" Her eyes roamed around us and onto Leon who was on his cell phone in an educated argument with someone. From the energy that he displayed it was clear that he was upset and losing this argument but he found the most effective way to camouflage his anger.

"Leon, I need you to come and sign this marriage license."

"Okay nephew I'll be right there." He replied. But he continued to bow down to whoever was on the other end.

"Babe I need your support." Teri whispered with my hand in hers. My antennas immediately went up and I was tuned in like Hot 97.

"Babe look at me." Mind you reader, I have been glaring into her eyes since she's gotten my attention and continued as she began to stress her overweight issue. For years Teri had the tendency to pity herself for the necessities that she feels she haven't been giving herself.

"I need you to help me get this weight off me. I need to be Pretty for you. I want to be able to get into that Beautiful White gown on our special day." As she expressed herself, I continued to be a listening ear for my soon to be wife.

"This is a serious situation babe. When I get like this I shut down in totality. I mean everything shuts down." She added. I pulled her to me and began to pray as I held her into my embrace.

"Lord I ask that you move through this woman's body. For she's a praying woman Lord God. I ask that you aid her in this situation." Immediately Teri began to verbally add to her regimen diet of Dos and DON'Ts.

Dos: Water, Fruits and Vegetables, Lean protein, Tea, Linguine, Apple cider vinegar, Honey, Oatmeal, Nuts, Boiled eggs, Fruit smoothie, Fish, Chicken breast…

Don'ts: Sugar, Added salt, Fast food, Fried food, Excessive coffee, Pastas, Rice, Cold cuts, Bread (Excess), Bacon and sausage, Potatoes, and No caffeine after 12 pm…

(Weekly grocery list)

Apples/Banana, Salad, Tomato, Cucumber, Salmon, Chicken, H2O, Lentils, Nuts, Eggs, Spinach, Protein Shakes. So on and so forth.... She was what one would consider A Speak it into existence type of female. This was ended with a Prayer of encouragement.

"Lord I need you in every area of my life. I can't make it without you. Please crucify my flesh daily to take excellent care of the body you have given me. I know my ministry, my life, my future marriage and my career depends on my health inside and out. Amen in Jesus name I pray.

"Okay you're all done. I will need you to bring this back signed by the Person that will be marrying you guys."

"Thank you, and enjoy the remainder of your day ma'am." Teri extended the gratitude. My Teri was over joyed.

Chapter Seventeen

It's Christmas season. As I passed the flower shop on Highway 27 South, with my Lord and savior's Jesus Christ Birthday being only weeks away, I decided that it was time that we have the Christmas spirit roaming around the house. So I pulled over and after an indecisive conversation, a 6 feet tree became a part of our household.

The tree brought a sense of joyfulness into the home. And before I knew it the girls were running around like chickens with their heads cut off. They were sneaking things into closets, leaving things in the trunk of the cars. They even had a gift or two in the back seat. As if we didn't know.

Before the day ended the tree had a skirt of presents surrounding it. I was shocked to see gifts labeled with me and mommy's name. Like last year this was a Christmas to remember. Only this time it was all smiles of innocence. Compared to the sorrow of waking up to the comfort of a vehicle covered with a thick blanket of snow.

REMINISCING..........

"Wow!!" I thought as the snow packed onto the front windshield. Never in a million years would a person think that Jack "The Pen" Hoagalino would be making a home out of the same vehicle that he used to transport people to and from. I looked in the driver's side mirror and as I attempted to wipe the boogers (Cold) from the corner of my eye, it was impossible to stop the flow of Cry water.

For the first time ever, I smelled the scent of stink rising from my body to the nostrils of my nose. After barely being able to push the door open through the thick snow. I figured that being that my mother lived in the building of the parking lot that I've been discreetly sleeping in, upset with her and all, I would go to her house to shower. I walked through the door and the holiday spirit ran through my body like the Holy spirit.

"Hey Bakann" I spoke to my mother. She returned the greeting and embraced me. I knew my mother smelled me and when my sister came from the back room it confirmed that I carried an odor that a person wouldn't want their pet to carry.

"Boy you stink!" Snarled my sister. Embarrassment would have been an understatement reader. I felt worse than a Billionaire who has gone bankrupt.

There was no comeback for this one. I looked at her and whispered "Is this the way a Christian woman treat a homeless person. Her cheerful facial express read that she didn't believe me. But when she read mine a tear rolled down her shiny cheeks.

"Boy why you didn't come here?" My mother questioned. Nor she or my sister would understand that this is part of the process of the shift that is taking place in my life. And I had to go through this to prep me for what lies ahead. Besides at 40 years of age what responsible man lives under the same roof as his mother? Unless it was she that needed shelter!

God made it possible because he knew that I was strong enough to not only go through, but make it out. This was the harsh truth of my reality. To God be the Glory!!!

"But thank God this Christmas will be in the comfort of family and a place that I can call Home.

Chapter Eighteen

"Yo I need you to be there 6 o'clock sharp." I told my Uncle Big. My fiancée was a little uneasy about us having him be the photographer. She was more like the KEEP YA FAMILY AND BUSINESS COMPLETELY SEPARATED! Type. But she had faith in my confidence so she let it play out.

"I'm so excited babe." I was excited that my lady was excited. I ran to the barbershop to get my edge up from my Uncle Leon.

"Leon just follow the line." I instructed him. Although Leon has been into the barbering business since a youth, one still had to be careful when they sat in his chair. You might go to get an edge-up and leave with a color disfiguration on the top of your head. So I made it clear every time I sat in his chair.

"I got you neph." He whispered. He then wrapped the cape around my neck and proceeded to cut my hair.

"Jack I heard you were getting married. Brother ain't get an invite or nothing."

"It will be small Ab." I told him. And it was the truth. My lady didn't want this to be a big broadcast for all to come and share with us. So we chose a select few. And Ab wouldn't be included in this small gathering.

"I'm just messing with you brah!" He countered. We both shared a light chuckle. Although he said this in a joking manner I felt the energy that he attempted to camouflage. Because being that we ran into each other in the shop daily, he probably felt as if we had the relationship that could at least get him to the ceremony, if nothing else. I'm not saying that we are not cool, his presence is just not needed at the union.

Now in the mirror mentally critiquing my edge up, I found myself zeroed in on the full beard. Leon actually did a good job this time reader. I put a small tip in his hand and rushed out of there to get to my future wife.

I walked through the door of my home and she and the girls were getting all pretty and stuff. My fiancé was the most Beautiful woman in the world. I only had eyes for her.

"Be ready in a minute babe." I ran to the bathroom with intentions of taking a bird bath. Once I close the door behind me something came over me. Tears began to uncontrollably roll down my face. Reader, it's like the more I wiped the more they force fed my pores, my beard and now they were dripping from my bearded chin.

I knew that I was making the right decision. But it was a big decision. Probably the biggest decision that I had to make in my entire life. Not to mention the leap from Jersey to Georgia we are about to take on faith alone. Things began to attack from every angle. First it was the Car troubles, then it was the lack of Documents for the house, and Money is always an issue of course. For some reason I felt cold feet. So for confirmation and stability I had to have a conversation with my God.

"My God!" I began to pray. Lord I need you to help me get through this.

Lord I'm so close yet my feet are so cold. I would love for You to make this transition easy on me and my family. But I rather ask that You provide me with the tools and the know how to proceed with this jump. Soon I will be a married man. And will begin a new life in a place that's like another world for me."

"Lord in Proverbs18:22 Your Word says; HE THAT FINDS A WIFE FINDS A GOOD THING AND OBTAINS FAVOR FROM THE LORD!!! Well Lord I know I ask for a lot and I don't want to be greedy but I ask for your Favor right now." Just then Teri placed her hands on my shoulder and whispered;

"Babe did Yolanda tell you about her revelation?"

"Revelation?" I questioned my future wife.

"I'm sorry babe, I think I'll let her tell you herself." Reader if you're anything like The Pen it irritates you when someone does this. But okay!

I looked in Yolanda's room and she was nowhere in sight.

"So where is Yolanda?" I asked Teri.

"She and Isha had to run to the store." She replied. So for the next 30 minutes I impatiently waited for my step-daughter to come home. 6:45 pm Isha walks through the door. Guess who's tagging along?!

"Hey Jack a riah!" They chimed. I gave them a little time to get settled in.

"So Yolanda, are you ready to tell me about your revelation?" I asked.

"Huh?" Was her response. She then looked at Teri who was carrying a sneaky grin across her face.

"Well since the cat is out of the bag, Mom." She whispered with an innocent glare.

"In case you don't know I have this fear for water."

"Right right" I shook in agreement.

"For some reason, I tend to dream-well have nightmares about Tsunamis."

"Anyway, I don't know the exact geographical location; (Pause) NOTE: Yolanda is always so politically correct reader. Continue:

"Country, State or wherever, but there was a Tsunami. A big Tsunami and like my other nightmares my first instinct was to run. But buildings popped up out of nowhere. So I grabbed a hold and began to latch on as if I were Spiderman.

I climbed and I leaped from building to building as they sunk into the Tsunami. But I never looked back. Instead I kept leaping from building to building with no fear that I would get caught in the Ocean of water."

"The message I got from this dream is; Even when you feel like it's too big of an obstacle don't give up. Make your obstacles go around you instead of you bowing down to your obstacles." She expressed.

"Reader I was in awe. This was my confirmation, because I tend to get cold feet during the times of adversities. My tears began to dry up on my face because I knew it was God alone who spoke through my step-daughter to toughen me up to better prepare me for this Shift!

"Hey babe, I'm about to be Mrs. Jack Hoagalino!" Like always she was so excited. And the faces that the girls displayed said that they were on one accord and pleased with this union.

Chapter Nineteen

"Okay babe, this is do or die." Teri whispered as we stood outside of the Church double doors. She stood in front of me, grabbed hold of both my hands. And we began to pray and pray until tears drenched both our faces. When we opened our eyes Big was posted up with the eye of the camera zeroed in on the both of us.

"Yes! Yes! Yes! Yes!" Pastor Bellamy screamed as we made our way to the altar. The Church was partially filled with family and friends.

As Pastor Bellamy began to read out of the Bible the instructions of becoming one, we searched each other's eyes and tears began to flow like a river. Together we agreed to become one and was happy with no ceremony or nothing. This marriage was long overdue. But filled with Glory in the eyesight of God we were now one. And from this First day of November in the year Two thousand and sixteenth day on, there was no turning back...

Chapter Twenty

"Big what up?" I greeted my Photographer. You called just in time. What's up with the pictures?" It has been over a month since the wife and I made it official as becoming one. We have been patiently waiting for the pictures to be produced.

"I don't want to jump the gun but for some reason we are still waiting." I told him.

With Big R being a family member, I figure this is typical family stuff. (You know the whole I got you! Just let me take care of this other guy first! Chill this is why I gave you the family discount, Family stuff!)

"I got this wedding to do. I also got a Birthday party to do. and still have to go to work." My Hitta what does that have to do with me? Is what I was thinking. As I thought this... my Teri voiced it. I just smiled.

"I mean I'm not trying to put y'all on the backburner Mrs. Hoagalino," He said with emphasis. But I have other things to handle than y'all pictures."

Speaking to Big is like speaking to the door. Unlike most guys, This guy is so cocky that he tries to convince you to believe that whatever he brings to the table is absolute correct. So I just let him be correct. (In his own mind) As long as his being correct doesn't put my lifetime memory in vain.

"Okay I guess my question should have been when will we be getting the pictures?" For about 30 seconds he became voiceless.

"I was calling to get more info from y'all. I have an idea. I need you to speak over your wife picture." I'm lost reader. The speaking over my Teri picture thing was way over the top. Not to mention, wherever it is he was going with this.

"Okay well I would have to speak to my Teri." After a brief silence;

"Well isn't your wife right there?"

"It's not that easy as you and Rachel may have it. Our agreements determine more than a yes and no thing. We must put more than just an answer in. You're talking about a life time memory here!" I told him.

"Okay holler at me when you know what you want to do." Inside I felt a little chuckle. By this time my Teri was returning from the kitchen.

"Somebody looks hungry!" She chimed with that signature smile.

The last Chapter

It Christmas day. After making it home from a rewarding night at Rockefeller Center we were shocked to see everything destroyed by water. Everything in the house was flooded. I was stuck on stupid. Didn't know where to begin. The wife and kids just stood in awe. Everyone's mind was somewhere else. Something had to be done, but how?

"I grabbed my wife hand and she grabbed the kid's hands and I began to pray like never before.

"Lord God what did we do to deserve this? Daily I raise Your name in Prayer. I help the ones that I can. I don't hang out, Drink, involve myself in Drugs, I have changed my life in ways that most would've only dreamed or prayed for. I need a miracle Lord God. Come into my home and move like never before! Move Lord Move!"

Immediately I called the office to complain about the incident. That morning they sent someone out to get the water up and help us save some of the things that were damaged. But to no avail, trying to save personal property from toilet water is like eating out of the garbage. So we began to get rid of things.

"I'm sorry about ya loss Cuz, do you have Home owner's insurance?"

"Home owner's insurance?" I questioned. Meanwhile my daughter was on the phone with someone.

"The lady is telling me that we have Home owner's insurance on our policy." I listened to my step-daughter and reported the damages to the lady who held the title as Claim specialist.

"I'm sorry for your loss, we will send an adjuster out Monday to view the damages. Meanwhile we will put you and your family up for the weekend."

Less than a week later an undisclosed amount was ACV'd to my account. "To God be the Glory!" Was all I could mustard up! Let's go...

Conclusion;

When God says that it's time to go. It's time to go!! God has already ordered your steps before giving you the order to make the move.

Success is not a Given! Sometimes we have to step outside of our element to obtain this...

Coming soon:

DA HARSH TRUTH

By: Zachery A. Hoagland

Later that night during Church service. The Spirit of the Lord was having its way with the Men and Women of God. I sat back and began to praise God for the countless blessings that has been coming our way. Then it happened.

"Jack take three steps towards this altar." I got up and pardon me, excused me, my way through the aisle until I made it to the altar.

"Give me your hand." He commanded. He then grabbed hold of my hand and began to walk with me across the front of the altar;

"I know how you feel, Jack. I know your thoughts. You will be a million miles away from home. You won't know anyone in Atlanta. And a bunch of other things that the devil is whispering in your ear."

"But the Lord said to tell you, just as I hold your hand, He will be there to hold your hand and walk with you. He said to tell you to follow your dream, to have no fear and that He will be with you holding your hand the whole step of the way."

Acknowledgements

First, I would like to thank my God for giving me the vision to see the possibility, the confirmation that it's real and the tools to aid me and my family to make such a move.

I would like to thank my Wife for inspiring me to move forward and follow the heart of my dream. I would like to thank her for critiquing each chapter as I wrote them. I Love you sweetheart.

I would like to thank my team: for motivating me by chasing me away. Special thanks to Daisy for giving me the name of THE SHIFT.

Oh, I DO NOT apologize for chasing you guys down. Lol. And forcing you guys to listen to how the book was turning out.

My mother Roxanne E. Hoagland for mothering such a creation. I love you and my sister. I heard you baby Ju'sarah Uncle Love you too...

My Pastor Lois Ballamy for the years the months the weeks she prayed over my life. The weeks that I missed service Members would tell me how Pastor would yell over the mic:

"Has anybody seen Zachery Hoagland?" Then begin to pray over my life. Also for solidifying me and the Wife's union. My cousin Jr. Pastor Justin Coleman for aiding and Touching and Agreeing with me.

My boy Bob and the team at Edison auto sales. Located in Edison, New Jersey off Route 1. For putting me in my very first BMW. This may not be much to you reader, but to have a stranger trust a stranger with bad credit to make payments says a lot.

NOTE: When/If you decide to visit my dealer, just say my name and you will leave off the lot with something worth your money. FACTS!!!!

I thank you my social media friends; Facebook, Instagram and Twitter for walking this life with ya boy Jack The Pen Hoagalino. Family and Friends you are who you are.

Thank you all! Love you all...

Last but not least Mr. Tyler Perry in advance for taking a chance with my dream. I look forward to meeting you.

Contact Info:

WEBSITE: Jackhoagalino.com

(732) 309-0208

FACEBOOK: Zachery Hoagland

INSTAGRAM: Zachery Hoagland

Twitter: @_Zhoagland